Balloon Tricks

Contents

Trick 1: Balloon lift — 4
Trick 2: Balloon-powered speedboat — 8
Trick 3: Screeching balloon — 12
Three balloon tricks — 22

Written by Becca Heddle
Illustrated by Chellie Carroll

Collins

Trick 1: Balloon lift

Start with a balloon in a cup.

Pump air into the balloon.

Let's explain!

The balloon expands and fills the cup. The cup squeezes the balloon in and keeps it tight.

When you lift the balloon, the cup lifts too!

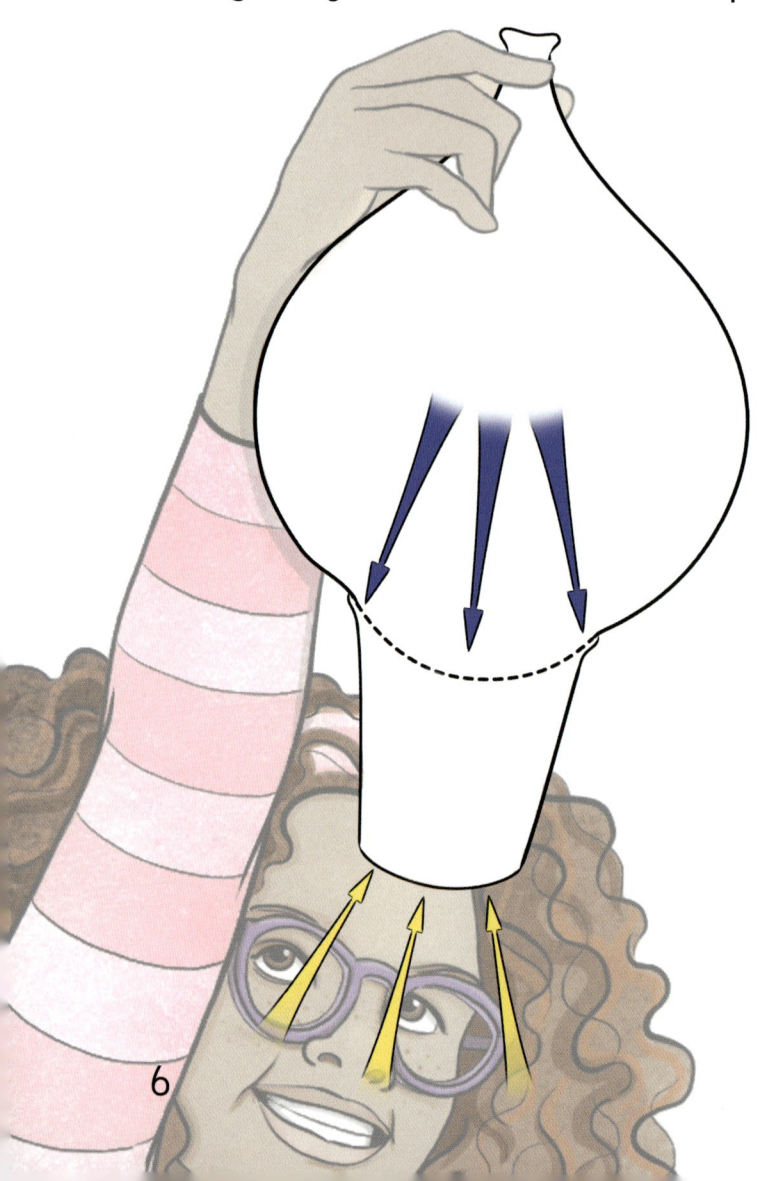

When you stop pinching, air spurts out.
The balloon shrinks, and the cup drops.

Trick 2: Balloon-powered speedboat

A balloon can power this speedboat!

Pump up the balloon.

Important! This must be tight.

Pinch the end to keep the air in.

Float the speedboat in a full container. Point it to a clear gap.

Let go. It speeds across the container!

Let's explain!

Air bursts out of the balloon.

The spurting air pushes the boat along.

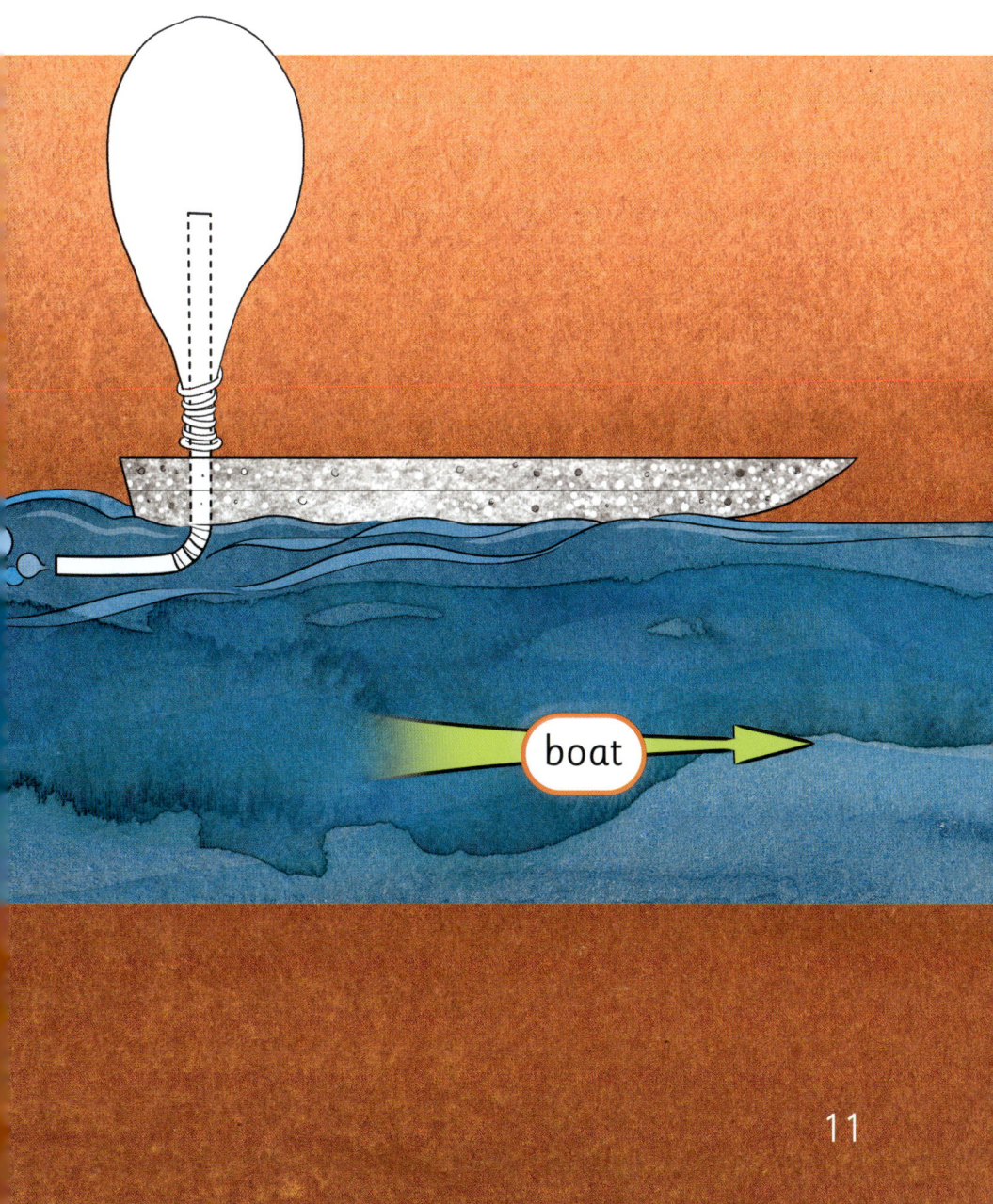

Trick 3: Screeching balloon

Start with a pumped-up balloon.

Pull the neck tight and let the air swoosh out. Hear the balloon screech!

Let's explain!

The screeching comes from the air squeezing out of the balloon's neck.

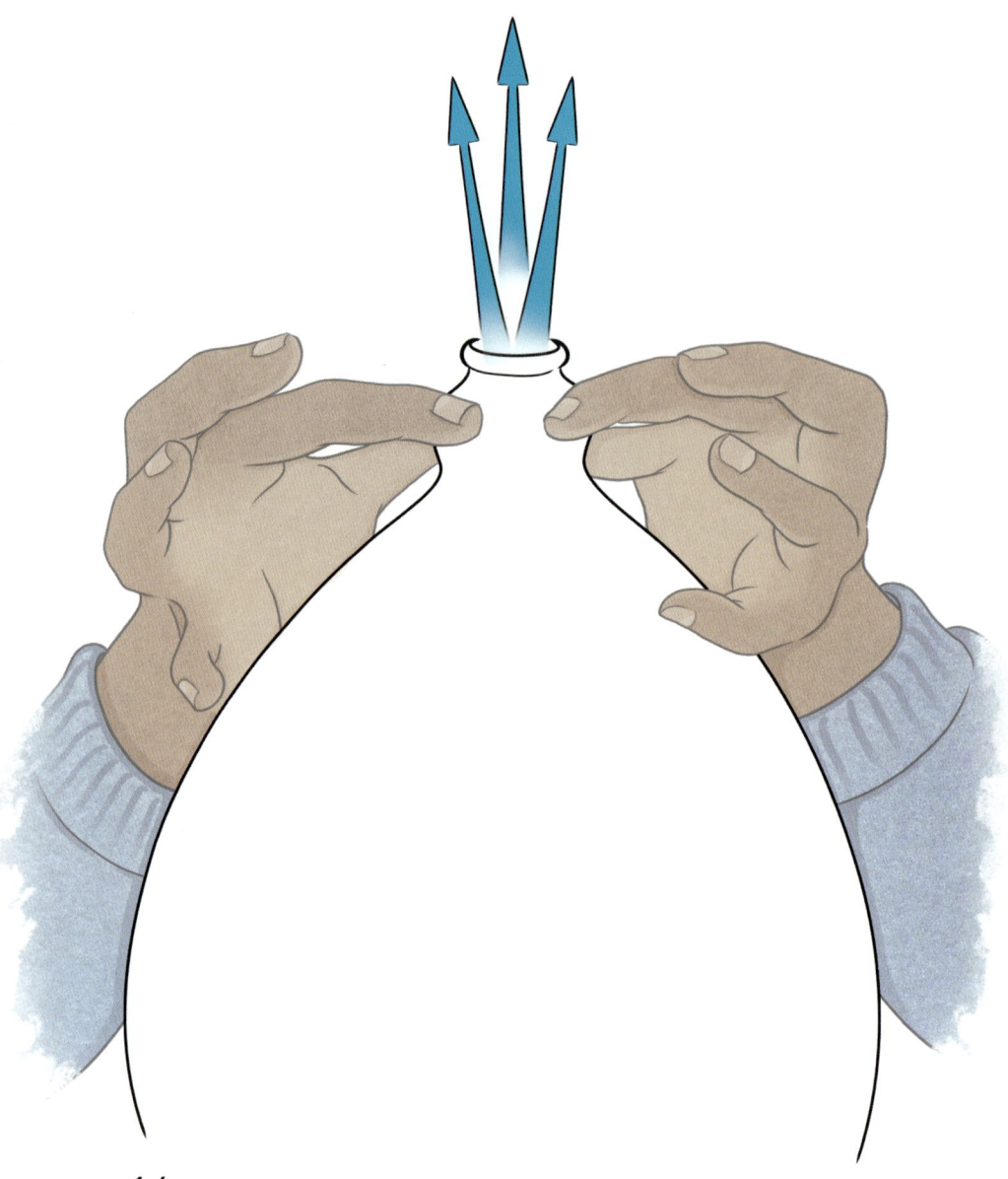

Pull the balloon's neck tighter. Hear how the screeches differ!

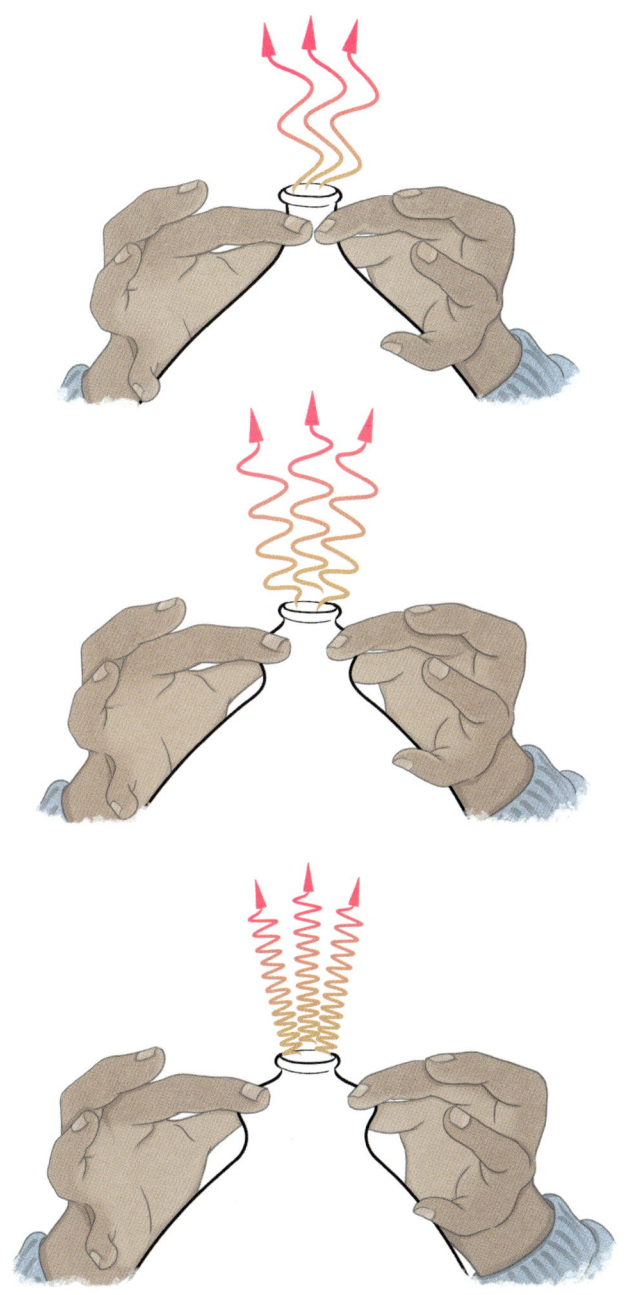

We can do lots of things with balloons. They can lift cups, power boats and screech!

That is proof that balloons are fantastic!

Hot-air balloons

This hot-air balloon floats high in the air. The burner gets the air in the balloon hot.

The hot air is light, so the balloon lifts up.

Rockets

In a rocket, burning gases push down, so the rocket can lift off.

The burning gases send the rocket into flight.

Three balloon tricks

23

Review: After reading

Use your assessment from hearing the children read to choose any words or tricky words that need additional practice.

Read 1: Decoding
- Focus on words with long vowel sounds and adjacent consonants. Ask the children to sound out and blend these longer words:
  screeching (*s/c/r/ee/ch/i/ng*)   **important** (*i/m/p/or/t/a/n/t*)
  squeezes (*s/qu/ee/z/e/s*)
- Ask the children to read pages 6 and 7. Encourage them to blend in their heads, silently, before reading the words aloud. Focus on the meaning of **expands** on page 6. Ask: What word on page 7 means the opposite of this? (**shrinks**)
- Bonus content: Challenge the children to read pages 18 and 19 fluently without sounding out. Say: Can you blend in your head when you read the words?

Read 2: Prosody
- Turn to pages 4 and 5. Discuss how you would read these pages if you were a scientist on a children's programme.
  - On page 4, ask: Which words are the most important to emphasise? (e.g. **start**, **balloon**, **cup**, **pump**)
  - Focus on page 5. What tone can we use to add excitement in the first sentence? (e.g. *surprise*, *encouragement*) Point out the exclamation mark.
  - Discuss which words to emphasise in the star-shaped panel. (e.g. **important**, **keep**)

Read 3: Comprehension
- Ask the children to describe where they have seen balloons. Talk about what balloons feel like and what they can do.
- Reread the opening sentence on page 2. Ask the children why the author thinks this. Encourage the children to back up their answer by referring to information or vocabulary in the book.
- Use the pictures on pages 22 and 23 as prompts to talk about each of the tricks. For each trick, ask: Can you explain why it works? Are there any important things we should be careful of when we do this trick?
- Bonus content: Turn to pages 20 and 21. Challenge the children to explain what makes the rocket lift off.